Nicola Phillipson TEP is a private client barrister at Parklane Plowden Chambers in Leeds whose practice encompasses probate and inheritance disputes. Nicola also sits as a Recorder and a Deputy District Judge on the North Eastern Circuit, and is a full member of STEP (Society of Trusts and Estate Practitioners). In 2020 Nicola was recognised as a Leading Junior by Legal 500 and was ranked in Band 2 in Chambers and Partners.

A Practical Guide to the Law in Relation to Control of the Body After Death

A Practical Guide to the Law in Relation to Control of the Body After Death

Nicola Phillipson TEP
Barrister
Parklane Plowden Chambers, Leeds
MA (Hons) (Oxon) Jurisprudence

Law Brief Publishing

Published 2020 by Law Brief Publishing, an imprint of Law Brief Publishing Ltd
30 The Parks
Minehead
Somerset
TA24 8BT

www.lawbriefpublishing.com

Paperback: 978-1-912687-98-5

In memory of John M. Collins, whose vast knowledge, endless patience, and good humour was appreciated by all who knew him, and without whom I would never have become a probate practitioner.

CONTENTS

INTRODUCTION

This a somewhat niche book on a niche subject, but it's an important subject, and one which tends to cause great emotion in clients. It is also an area of law where time is of the essence, so it is intended that this book will be a valuable guide to the busy practitioner when faced with a dispute over a body.

As a practical text book, I make no apologies for the duplication in the chapters – this is deliberate so that you only need to look at the relevant chapter for your particular query and you don't have to read three different chapters to check that you haven't missed anything.

This is a book aimed at probate practitioners, and it therefore assumes a basic working knowledge of the law in this area (eg, the difference between executors and administrators etc..). I use 'Personal Representative' throughout except where there is a difference between executors and administrators, where I differentiate.

I had to draw the line somewhere, so this book does not cover the practice and procedure of actually disposing of a body (ie, the forms needed for burial, cremation etc…). The book does however cover the following:

1. Possession of the Body – this chapter notes that there is no property in a body and therefore considers who has a duty to dispose of the body and therefore has a corresponding right to possession of the same. This chapter also briefly covers the provisions of the Human Tissue Act 2004 in relation to the issue of who can lay claim to the body.

2. The Duty to Properly Dispose of a Body – what does the duty to 'properly dispose' of the body entail, and to what extent are the wishes of the Testator binding?

3. Applications to the Court (Practice and Procedure) – this chapter looks at the authority of the court to decide who should be given the duty to dispose of the body, and the applications which can be made.

4. Applications to the Court (Factors for the Court to Consider) - Having made the application to the court, what are the factors the court will consider when deciding to whom the duty to dispose of the body should be given?

5. Funeral and Disposal Disputes – how far can the Testator, family members, or the court, interfere with the right of the person with the duty to dispose of the body to decide upon the method of disposal and any funeral?

6. Ashes and Cremation – a chapter considering cremation of the body and arguments over the ashes.

7. Exhumation of Bodies and Ashes – an overview of exhumation of bodies and ashes.

8. Headstones and Memorials – although not technically a dispute over a body, this chapter considers who has the right to erect headstones and other memorials to the Deceased.

9. Costs – a very short two paragraphs on costs which has only been given its own chapter so it can be found easily.

The law stated in this book is believed to be accurate and up-to-date as of 20/09/2020.

CHAPTER ONE
POSSESSION OF THE BODY

> "There is no right of ownership in a dead body. However, there is a duty at common law to arrange for its proper disposal. This duty falls primarily upon the personal representatives of the deceased (see *Williams v. Williams* (1881) 20 Ch. 659; *Rees v. Hughes* [1946] K.B. 517). An executor appointed by will is entitled to obtain possession of the body for that purpose (see *Sharp v. Lush* (1879) 10 Ch. 468 at 472; *Dobson v. North Tyneside Health Authority* [1997] 1 WLR 596 at 600 obiter), even before there has been a grant of Probate. Where there is no executor that same duty falls upon the administrators of the estate, but they may not be able to obtain an injunction for delivery of the body before the grant of letters of administration (see *Dobson*)."
>
> – *Buchanan v Milton*[1] per Hale J.

This oft quoted extract from *Buchanan* clearly and succinctly sets out the law in relation to the issue of who has the 'right' to possession of a body after death. A dead body cannot be classed as 'property' and therefore cannot be owned by anyone after death. There is, however, a duty to ensure that the body is properly disposed of, and the person/body tasked with this duty has the corresponding right to call for possession of the body to enable this duty to be fulfilled.

---

1 [1999] 2 FLR 844

It can therefore be seen that to answer the question 'who is entitled to the body after death?', the question which generally needs to be asked is actually 'who has the duty to properly dispose of the body?' Absent an order from the court, the order of priority for those with the duty to dispose of the body is as follows:

i. where there is a valid will – the executor(s) named in the will.

ii. Where there is an intestacy, the administrator(s) named on the letters of administration.

iii. Where there is an intestacy but Personal Representatives have not been appointed, it will be the person(s) with the highest right to take out a grant as set out in section 46 of the Administration of Estates Act 1925 and rule 22.1 of the Non-Contentious Probate Rules 1987.

Non-Contentious Probate Rules 1987 SI 2024, Rule 22.1:

22.— Order of priority for grant in case of intestacy

(1) Where the deceased died on or after 1st January 1926, wholly intestate, the person or persons having a beneficial interest in the estate shall be entitled to a grant of administration in the following classes in order of priority, namely–

(a) the surviving spouse or civil partner;

(b) the children of the deceased and the issue of any deceased child who died before the

deceased;

(c) the father and mother of the deceased;

(d) brothers and sisters of the whole blood and the issue of any deceased brother or sister

of the whole blood who died before the deceased;

(e) brothers and sisters of the half blood and the issue of any deceased brother or sister of

the half blood who died before the deceased;

(f) grandparents;

(g) uncles and aunts of the whole blood and the issue of any deceased uncle or aunt of the

whole blood who died before the deceased;

(h) uncles and aunts of the half blood and the issue of any deceased uncle or aunt of the

half blood who died before the deceased.

iv. The householder in whose property the Deceased died[2] and/or the person with actual possession of the body (often a hospital or the coroner).

v. In the absence of any of the above, section 46 of the Public Health (Control of Disease) 1984 provides that it shall be the duty of a local authority to cause to be buried or cremated the body of any person who has died or been found dead in their area, in any case where it appears to the authority that no suitable arrangements for the disposal of the body have

2 *Re: Stewart* 12 Ad & El 773

> been or are being made otherwise than by the authority. An authority shall not cause a body to be cremated where they have reason to believe that cremation would be contrary to the wishes of the deceased, and an authority may recover the expenses from the estate of the deceased person.

In relation to children, if the child is in the care of the Local Authority, following the death of the child, the right or duty to dispose of the body reverts to the child's natural (or adopted) parents (*R v Gwynedd County Council ex parte B*[3]).

It can be seen that the list of people with a 'duty to dispose' does not include 'a person nominated by the Testator'. As a body is not classed as 'property', a direction in a will as to the disposition of the Testator's body cannot be enforced[4]

Where a dispute arises between two or more people equally obliged to carry out the duty, or where there is a dispute between the person so obliged and other persons, an application can be made to the court to determine to whom a grant should be given for the purposes of disposing of the body[5].

It is sometimes said that where there is no executor, possession of the body will belong to the next of kin. However, in *Dobson v. North Tyneside Health Authority*[6], it was noted that although the Personal Representatives of the Deceased and those who have a duty to inter the Deceased, have the right to custody and possession of the body until the duty is discharged, the court was "not aware that there is

---

3 [1992] 3 All ER 317

4 *Williams v. Williams* (1881) 20 Ch. 659

5 see Chapter 3

6 [1997] 1 WLR 596

any authority that there is such a duty on the next of kin as such. If there is no duty, there is no legal right to possession of the corpse."

Where a coroner is under a duty to investigate the death of the Deceased, or is considering whether (s)he is under such a duty, the coroner has a right to possession of the body for that purpose[7], although the coroner must release the body for burial or cremation "as soon as is reasonably practicable" and notify the next of kin or Personal Representative of the Deceased of the reason for any delay beyond 28 days[8].

Exceptions

Having said that there is no property in a dead body, and that a Testator cannot dispose of his/her body by will, the potential exceptions to these rules must be considered. These exceptions concern bodies or body parts which have undergone a process of human application or skill and the provisions of the Human Tissue Act 2004 ("HTA").

Human Application or Skill

Bodies, or parts of bodies, are capable of being classed as property if they have acquired different attributes through the application of skill such as dissection or preservation techniques[9].

Giving judgment in *R v Kelly*, Rose LJ stated that "it has now been the common law for 150 years at least that neither a corpse nor part

7 section 15 of the Coroners and Justice Act 2009

8 Coroners (Investigations) Regulations 2013 (SI 2013/1629), Regulation 20.

9 *R v Kelly* [1999] QB 621

of a corpse are in themselves and without more capable of being property protected by rights", and it is noted that the offence of removing a body from a grave is to be distinguished from theft of a corpse. "If that principle is now to be changed, in our view, it must be by Parliament …". It is however also noted that the common law does not stand still, and therefore it may be that in the future, if the occasion arises, the court will hold that human body parts are capable of being property for the purposes of s.4[10] even without the acquisition of different attributes, if they have a use or significance beyond their mere existence – for example, intended for use in an organ transplant operation, for the extraction of DNA, or as an exhibit in a trial.

In *Dobson v. North Tyneside Health Authority*[11], it was held that the removal of a brain and preserving the same in paraffin as part of a post mortem did not have the effect of transforming the brain into an item to which the Claimant, in circumstances where she had no duty to dispose of the body, had a right of possession.

Human Tissue Act 2004 ("HTA")

The HTA is a statutory scheme which permits, either by will or other appropriate consent[12], the donation of a body, organs and/or tissue for the purposes set out in Schedule 1 of the HTA, which include research, transplantation and public display. This scheme operates as an exception to the rule that instructions given by the Deceased as to how his/her body should be dealt with after death are not binding. The HTA Code of Practice A[13] provides:

10 of the Theft Act 1968

11 [1997] 1 WLR 596

12 HTA s.3

13 The current version was published 20 May 2020

> 20. If appropriate and valid consent has been provided, then this is sufficient for an activity covered by the HT Act to proceed (subject to licensing and other legislative requirements having been met).
>
> 21. The existence of consent permits an activity to proceed, but does not mandate that it must. However, once someone has given consent, no other person has a legal right to revoke it and the decision whether to proceed with an activity rests with the person who will be undertaking it. The HT Act and common law establish the principle that the decision to consent rests first and foremost with the person whose body, organ, tissues or cells are being used. Where that person has died, their nominated representatives or relatives should be sensitively supported to respect that person's consent to ensure the best chance of their wishes being fulfilled.

The intricacies of the HTA are beyond the scope of this work, but it should be noted that by section 4 of the HTA, an adult may appoint one or more nominated representatives to carry out his/her wishes after death in relation to activities for which consent under the HTA is required. Such representative will not necessarily be the Personal Representative.

The HTA also provides that consent can be given by a child or a person who had parental responsibility for the child immediately before the child's death[14], which person may of course not be the natural or adopted parent of the child. In relation to children, the Code of Practice A states:

---

14 s.2

> 87. Under the HT Act, a child (except in the context of qualifying relationships) is defined as being under 18 years old. The position of a child who, before they died, was competent to reach a decision and gave consent for one or more scheduled purposes after their death, is no different from that of an adult. Their consent is sufficient for medical practitioners to make lawful under the HT Act the removal, storage or use of tissue for the specified scheduled purpose(s). Additional requirements may apply under other legislation. For example, clinical research may also be regulated by the Medicines and Healthcare products Regulatory Agency (MHRA) and clinical trials regulations.
>
> 88. The principle of 'Gillick competence' applies to the assessment of a child's competence to consent in these circumstances. In the Gillick case, the court held that a child was considered competent to give valid consent to a proposed intervention if they had sufficient intelligence and understanding to enable them to fully understand what was involved.

It can therefore be seen that the HTA provides scope for a situation where there may be an argument that a nominated representative under the HTA, or a person with parental responsibility for a child, has a greater call on the body than the Personal Representative.

Court Orders

As will be considered in later chapters, the court has the power to disrupt the hierarchy of those entitled to call for the body, and has even dictated precisely how a body will be disposed of[15]. The court also has inherent power to direct DNA testing post mortem of extracted DNA samples to establish biological relationships, regardless of the wishes of the Personal Representative[16].

---

15 *Oldham Metropolitan Borough Council v Makin* [2017] EWHC 2543 (Ch)

16 *Spencer v Spencer* [2018] EWCA Civ 100 (also known as *Anderson v Spencer*) See also *Nield-Moir v Freeman* [2018] EWHC 299 (Ch) where HHJ Matthews suggested at paragraph 36 that the court "may well have an inherent jurisdiction to order a person to consent to giving such a sample so that it may be DNA tested. A failure in such a case to consent might then amount to a contempt of court".

CHAPTER TWO
THE DUTY TO PROPERLY DISPOSE OF A BODY

As was said by Hale J in *Buchanan v Milton*[1], although there is no right of ownership in a dead body, there is a duty at common law to arrange for its proper disposal. As was seen in Chapter 2, this duty falls upon the following people in the following order:

i. Where there is a valid will – the executor(s) named in the will.

ii. Where there is an intestacy, the administrator(s) named on the letters of administration.

iii. Where there is an intestacy but Personal Representatives have not been appointed, it will be the person(s) with the highest right to take out a grant as set out in section 46 of the Administration of Estates Act 1925 and rule 22.1 of the Non-Contentious Probate Rules 1987.

iv. The householder in whose property the Deceased died[2] and/or the person with actual possession of the body (often a hospital or the coroner).

v. In the absence of any of the above, section 46 of the Public Health (Control of Disease) 1984 provides that it shall be the duty of a local authority to cause to be buried or cremated the body of any person who has died or been found dead in

---

1 [1999] 2 FLR 844

2 *Re: Stewart* 12 Ad & El 773

> their area, in any case where it appears to the authority that no suitable arrangements for the disposal of the body have been or are being made otherwise than by the authority. An authority shall not cause a body to be cremated where they have reason to believe that cremation would be contrary to the wishes of the deceased, and an authority may recover the expenses from the estate of the deceased person.

As a body is not classed as 'property' and therefore cannot be disposed of by will (*Williams v Williams*[3]), a Testator cannot upset this hierarchy of those with a 'duty to dispose' by nominating someone other than the Personal Representative to take possession of the body for the purposes of disposing of the same[4].

The duty to 'properly dispose' of the body, includes an obligation to ensure that the disposal takes place within a reasonable period taking into account all relevant factors"[5]. In the event that the Personal Representative does not arrange for the proper disposal in a timely manner, then whoever is 'currently in lawful possession of the body' has the power to make proper arrangements for the disposal.

In *Lakey v Medway Foundation Trust*[6], a Personal Representative had not disposed of the body of his late wife for over three years, as he believed that the body should be retained so as to be available for investigations and tests further to the Personal Representative's complaints as to how his wife was treated during her lifetime. The court gave the hospital trust, in whose morgue the body was lying, a Declaration that the trust was entitled to bury or cremate the body after giving seven days' notice to the Claimant.

3 (1881) 20 Ch. 659

4 But see the commentary on the Human Tissue Act 2004 at chapter 2

5 per Silber J in *Lakey v Medway Foundation Trust* [2009] EWHC 3574 (QB)

6 [2009] EWHC 3574 (QB)

In *re K (A Child) (Disposal of Body: Court's Power to Authorise)*[7], the High Court used its inherent jurisdiction to make an order authorising the local authority to assume responsibility for arranging and carrying out the disposal of K's body by way of burial or cremation, making the necessary funeral arrangements, and if the body was to be cremated, the disposal of the ashes. This was in circumstances where K had died in conditions suggesting non-accidental injury, and where neither parent had made any effort to arrange a funeral or for the respectful disposal of the body, despite the body having been released by the coroner several months earlier.

A further consequence of a body not being classed as 'property' is that a Testator cannot compel their Personal Representative to dispose of their body in a particular way[8]. As Jackson J confirmed in *In re JS (A child) (Disposal of Body: Prospective Orders)*[9];

> "in English law, there is no right to dictate the treatment of one's body after death. This is so regardless of testamentary capacity or religion. The wishes of the deceased are relevant, perhaps highly so, but are not determinative and cannot bind third parties."

In *Burrows v HM Coroner for Preston*[10] Cranston J found that, following jurisprudence from the European Courts of Human Rights, the common law rule that the views of a deceased person can be ignored, "is no longer good law"[11]. This assertion was, however, disputed in *Ibuna v Arroyo*[12] where Peter Smith J said:

---

7 [2017] 4 WLR 112 (Fam)

8 But see the commentary on the Human Tissue Act 2004 at chapter 2

9 [2016] EWHC 2859 (Fam)

10 [2008] EWHC 1387 (QB) also reported as *Borrows v HM Coroner for Preston*

11 at paragraph 20

12 [2012] EWHC 428 (Ch)

> "It seems to me that the established law is correctly summarised by Hale J as she then was in ***Buchanan*** which gives the executor the primary duty to dispose of the body. In disposing of the body the executor is entitled to have regard to the expression made by the deceased but is not bound by them. Given that principle in my view there is no room further for any application of any human rights concepts to protect the right of the body to speak from death as it were"[13]

The comments of Jackson J in *Re JS* post-date both *Burrows* and *Ibuna*, and can therefore be taken to reflect the correct interpretation of the rights of the Deceased *vis a vis* how the body should be properly disposed of; the decision as to how the body should be properly disposed of ultimately rests with the person who has the duty to carry out this task. Once the Personal Representative has established their right to dispose of a body, their discretion in this matter will not be interfered with by the court unless the Personal Representative has acted unreasonably:

> "To my mind it is plain that even if the performance of the executor's duty is capable of being controlled at the suit of a relative, the executor must have a discretion as to the mode and place for the disposal of the corpse of the Deceased and that on ordinary principles the court will not interfere with the exercise of that discretion unless it is exercised in a way which shows that he has not properly weighed the factors which ought to have been taken into account in that it is wholly unreasonable." [14]

13 at paragraph 50

14 *Grandison v Nembhard* 4 BMLR 140

CHAPTER THREE
APPLICATIONS TO THE COURT (PRACTICE AND PROCEDURE)

Where there is a dispute about the manner of disposal of a body, how to deal with the ashes, or the arrangements made for the funeral, there are a number of ways these matters can practically be put before the court for resolution.

The most common route is for one party to make an application to the court pursuant either to the High Court's inherent jurisdiction or to section 116 of the Senior Courts Act 1981 ("s.116"), asking the court to appoint a specified Personal Representative for the limited purpose of disposing of the body, dealing with the ashes or arranging the funeral etc.

s.116 provides:

> **Power of court to pass over prior claims to grant**
>
> (1) If by reason of any special circumstances it appears to the High Court to be necessary or expedient to appoint as administrator some person other than the person who, but for this section, would in accordance with probate rules have been entitled to the grant[1], the court may in its discretion appoint as administrator such person as it thinks expedient.
>
> (2) Any grant of administration under this section may be limited in any way the court thinks fit.

---

1 Note that r.20 Non-Contentious Probate Rules deals with order of priority for grant where the Deceased left a will. r.22 specifies the order of priority in case of intestacy

In *In re JS (A child) (Disposal of Body: Prospective Orders)*[2], Jackson J confirmed that s.116 could be used not only to appoint someone who would not otherwise have been entitled to the grant, but also to choose a Personal Representative from a class of persons all equally entitled, to the exclusion of the others. In this case JS was a terminally ill child who had clearly articulated her wishes that she wished her body to be cryo-preserved upon her death, and that her father, from whom she was estranged, should not be allowed to view her body after her passing. The parents, who were equally entitled to a grant upon the death of JS, disagreed as to honouring JS' wishes, and as a minor, JS could not make a will appointing her (supportive) mother as her executor. JS herself applied to the court for a determination that her wishes be adhered to on her death.

In the highly unusual circumstances of this case, Jackson J made a prospective order under s.116, alternatively under the inherent jurisdiction of the high court, to take effect upon JS' death, appointing the mother as the sole administrator in place of the mother and father jointly, and specifying that the mother should thereby have the right to make arrangements as to the disposal of JS' body and to decide who should be permitted to view it.

In *Anstey v Mundle*[3], heard seven months before *JS*, Mr Jonathan Klein had misgivings as to the use of s.116 to choose between persons equally entitled to a grant, and therefore preferred to rest his decision on the inherent jurisdiction of the court, noting that he would have reached the same decision in any event.

---

2 [2016] EWHC 2859 (Fam)

3 [2016] EWHC 1073

In *ND v LD*[4], Judge Gareth Jones noted that the decision of Jackson J in *Re JS* in relation to the use of s.116 was followed in *Re K*[5] by Hayden J, and Judge Jones accepted that s.116 does allow one administrator to be substituted for another, or for administrators acting jointly.

In *Jakimaviciut v HM Coroner for Westminster*[6], the court was asked to decide which of two sisters ought to have released to her, the body of their mother which was in the possession of the coroner. One sister was named as executor of her mother's will, the other had obtained letters of administration[7]. In the course of his judgment, Mr Mark Cawson QC noted:

> "34. Before a full grant of probate or letters of administration, it may be possible to place reliance on section 116 of the Senior Courts Act 1981 ... However, this does not provide assistance where, as in the present case, a full grant has been taken out and remains unrevoked, albeit challenged.
>
> 35. The authorities are, however, to the effect that the court has an inherent jurisdiction, existing as part of its jurisdiction over the administration of estates, to give directions concerning the release of a body to persons other than the named executor. The court has exercised this inherent jurisdiction in circumstances such as where there was a dispute between a mother and a father in respect of the body of their adult son (*Hartshorne v Gardner* [2008] 2 FLR 1681), or where there has been a dispute as to the validity of a will and thus as to the

4 [2019] EWHC 3639 (Fam)

5 [2018] 1 FLR 96

6 [2019] 10 WLUK 523

7 by swearing the oath that she was the daughter and "only person entitled to the estate of the said deceased"

identity executors, prima facie, entitled to the body (see *Anstey v Mundle*, [2016] EWHC 1073 (Ch)).

36. The existence of this inherent power or jurisdiction has been more recently confirmed in the case of *Oldham Metropolitan Borough Council v Makin* [2018] 543 (Ch), which was concerned with the question as to how the body of the Moors Murderer, Ian Brady, should be dealt with, …

37. In my judgment, there is no reason, in principle, why the inherent jurisdiction should not be exercised even where a full grant of probate or letters of administration has, as in the present case, been taken out. However, the court is likely to be slow in invoking this inherent jurisdiction as against an appointed personal representative, at least unless the grant itself is the subject of challenge. In the present case, proceedings are, as I have said, on foot in which the grant of letters of administration obtained by Lina is subject to challenge."

As an alternative to s.116 or the court's inherent jurisdiction, rule 27(6) of the Non-Contentious Probate Rules, provides that "A dispute between persons entitled to a grant in the same degree shall be brought by summons before a District Judge or a Registrar", and in the case of *Fessi v Whitmore*[8], the location for the scattering of the deceased's ashes was decided on the basis that the court was being asked to resolve a dispute between two trustees.

In circumstances where there is an executor, or where letters of administration have been granted, there would seem to be no reason why s.50 of the Administration of Justice Act 1985 ("s.50") could not be used:

8 [1999]1 FLR 767

50. Power of High Court to appoint substitute for, or to remove, personal representative.

(1) Where an application relating to the estate of a deceased person is made to the High Court under this subsection by or on behalf of a personal representative of the deceased or a beneficiary of the estate, the court may in its discretion —

(a) appoint a person (in this section called a substituted personal representative) to act as personal representative of the deceased in place of the existing personal representative or representatives of the deceased or any of them; or

(b) if there are two or more existing personal representatives of the deceased, terminate the appointment of one or more, but not all, of those persons.

(2) Where the court appoints a person to act as a substituted personal representative of a deceased person, then—

(a) if that person is appointed to act with an executor or executors the appointment shall (except for the purpose of including him in any chain of representation) constitute him executor of the deceased as from the date of the appointment; and

(b) in any other case the appointment shall constitute that person administrator of the deceased's estate as from the date of the appointment.

……

(5) In this section "beneficiary", in relation to the estate of a deceased person, means a person who under the will of the deceased or under the law relating to intestacy is beneficially interested in the estate.

It was confirmed in *Goodman v Goodman*[9] that the power under s.50 to remove or replace executors can be exercised both before and after a grant of probate.

s.50 has an advantage over s.116 in that the court requires there to be "special circumstances" under s.116 before the court can exercise discretion, whereas for s.50 the court simply needs an application. It is however noted that there is no power within s.50 to appoint the Personal Representative for limited purposes only, and it should also be remembered that the class of people who can apply under s.50 is limited to the Personal Representative or a beneficiary of the estate, although as s.56 of the Administration of Justice Act 1985 defines "will" as including a "nuncupative will and any testamentary document of which probate may be granted", where there are a number of wills and a potential intestacy, the class of eligible applicants may in fact be very wide.

There is conflicting authority as to whether the court can not only appoint a Personal Representative to make the arrangements for the proper disposal of the body and any attendant funeral, but whether it can also give directions as to the method of disposal and the manner in which any funeral should be held. In *Anstey v Mundle*[10], Jonathan Klein said that he did not think that the court can determine or direct where or how the Deceased should be buried; what the court can do is direct who has the power and duty to properly dispose of the Deceased[11]. In *Re JS*, Jackson J referred to *Anstey* and said that "the role of the court is not to give directions for the disposal of the body but to resolve disagreement about who may make the arrangements"[12]. However, in *Oldham Metropolitan Borough Council v*

9 [2013] EWHC 758 (Ch)

10 [2016] EWHC 1073 (Ch)

11 at paragraph 47

12 at paragraph 49

Makin[13], which was concerned with how the body of the Moors Murderer, Ian Brady, should be dealt with, the Chancellor, Sir Geoffrey Vos, referred to *Grandison v Nembhard*[14] and *Hartshorne v Gardner*[15] and found that the court had inherent jurisdiction to give directions as to the method by which a body should be disposed of, and proceeded to give precise directions for the same, even down to the issue of whether music could be played during the cremation.

Actual Procedure

Applications under s.116 are governed by rule 52 of the Non-Contentious Probate Rules which provides:

> **52. Grants of administration under discretionary powers of court, and grants ad colligenda bona**
>
> An application for an order for–
>
> (a) a grant of administration under section 116 of the Act; or
>
> (b) a grant of administration ad colligenda bona,
>
> may be made to a district judge or registrar and shall be supported by an affidavit setting out the grounds of the application.

As well as setting out the grounds of the application, the affidavit should provide details of the Deceased, those entitled to the estate, the gross and net value of the estate, those entitled to the grant (and their order of priority), the intended Personal Representative, and a

13 [2017] EWHC 2543 (Ch)

14 (1989) 4 BMLR 140

15 [2008] EWHC 3675 (Ch)

copy of any will should be exhibited. It is also good practice to include a statement confirming that the proposed Personal Representative is a fit and proper person[16].

An application under s.50 proceeds under the CPR (see CPR 57.13 and PD57 paragraphs 12 – 14).

16 This should be an independent statement, not from the applicant, *Long v Rodman* [2019] EWHC 753 (Ch)

CHAPTER FOUR
APPLICATIONS TO THE COURT (FACTORS FOR THE COURT TO CONSIDER)

Having made the application to the court to for a grant to enable a particular party to decide how a body should be disposed of[1], what factors will the court consider when deciding to whom the grant should be given? It must be accepted at the outset that all cases are very fact specific, and the approach of the court is necessarily different where it has only one party entitled to the grant, as opposed to having to decide between competing applicants who are equally entitled.

<u>Only one party entitled</u>

In *Holtham v Arnold*[2], Hoffman J had to decide whether the Deceased's estranged wife, or the Deceased's common law wife of two years, was entitled to arrange the Deceased's funeral. Having considered the evidence, the Judge found for the Deceased's estranged wife, on the basis that she was the party entitled to the letters of administration of the Deceased's estate.

"Looking at the evidence on both sides there seems to be no doubt that Mrs Holtham on one side and the family on the other both feel very strongly that it is their right and their duty to conduct the funeral. I think it is virtually impossible for a court to express any moral judgment as between them. The relationship between a man

---

1 see Chapter 3

2 (1986) 2 BMLR 123

in the position of Mr Arnold and Mrs Holtham on the one hand and his family on the other are in the nature of things extremely difficult for an outsider to penetrate. … Indeed I think it is a matter which it would be almost presumptuous to explore. In those circumstances the only course really open to the court is to decide the matter according to law; and the law, as I have said, is that the person lawfully entitled to administration has the duty to conduct the funeral."

The same approach was followed by Patten J in *Scotching v Birch*[3] where the dispute between the parents of the Deceased child centred around the location of the funeral and subsequent burial. At the time of the hearing, the mother was on remand awaiting trial for murder of the Deceased, her plea of guilty to manslaughter on the grounds of diminished responsibility having been rejected by the Crown. Patten J found that, given the public policy rule that prohibits a person who unlawfully kills another from taking a benefit under their Estate, the mother had no locus to apply for the grant under Rule 22(1) Non-Contentious Probate Rules. It was accepted that the Second to Fourth Defendants in this case, who were mother's minor children from a previous marriage, also had no locus. Patten J noted that both sides had genuine and serious interests and concerns and that "it is almost impossible to weigh up and decide between these various factors in purely qualitative terms", as would have been necessary under section 116[4]. However, the court was not called upon to do so in this case, as the matter was determined, as a matter of practicality, by the fact that the mother had no locus, "and without that the wider issues of discretion and a consideration of the effect on the other children do not really come into play". Limited letters of administration were therefore granted to the father.

---

3 [2008] EWHC 844

4 of the Senior Courts Act 1981

In *Lewisham Hospital v Hamuth*[5], the hospital householder under whose roof the Deceased had died (and also the party in actual possession of the body) was Declared to have the right to make the decision as to the appropriate arrangements for the disposal of the body in circumstances where the First Defendant was the executor appointed under a disputed will, and the Second to Thirteenth Defendants were either first or second cousins of the Deceased and there was a bona fide dispute over the validity of the will and therefore the appointment of the executor, which was highly unlikely to be resolved in the period of time during which arrangements for the disposal of the body will typically have to be made. The conclusion reached by Hart J was that as the hospital was in lawful possession of the body, and there was no way of resolving the executor dispute within an acceptable time period, the decision as to the disposal of the body should be left to the hospital.

The case of *Hamuth* was cited in *Laing v John Poyser Solicitors*[6] where the Court of Appeal declined to interfere with the First Instance decision of His Honour Judge Hodge who refused the injunction sought by the Deceased's son to prevent the solicitors, who had been named as executor in the will, from cremating the Deceased. The son disputed the validity of the will on the basis of lack of testamentary capacity. In his judgment refusing the injunction, HHJ Hodge had said that the court was not in a position to finally adjudicate upon the validity of the will or whether the Deceased wished to be buried or cremated. On the evidence, however, it could not be said that the challenge to the validity was certain to succeed. In dismissing the appeal, the Court of Appeal referred to *Hamuth*, and noted that in the present case, the Solicitors were in lawful possession of the body and therefore on the face of it, had the right and duty to make the arrangements.

5 [2006] EWHC 1609

6 [2012] EWCA Civ 1240

Parties equally entitled

Where a dispute cannot be decided on the basis of practicality, it will usually be the case that the court will have to consider the matter either pursuant to the provisions of section 116 of the Senior Courts Act 1981 ("s.116"), or alternatively under the inherent jurisdiction of the court.

s.116 provides:

> **Power of court to pass over prior claims to grant**
>
> (1) If by reason of any special circumstances it appears to the High Court to be necessary or expedient to appoint as administrator some person other than the person who, but for this section, would in accordance with probate rules have been entitled to the grant, the court may in its discretion appoint as administrator such person as it thinks expedient.
>
> (2) Any grant of administration under this section may be limited in any way the court thinks fit.

It was held in *Buchanan v Milton*[7], that when faced with a s.116 application, the court must first determine if there are special circumstances which justify passing over the person entitled to the grant in accordance with the probate rules[8]. The second stage is to decide whether, in light of those special circumstances, it is necessary or expedient for the court to vary the order of administration[9].

7 [1999] 2 FLR 844

8 Note that r.20 Non-Contentious Probate Rules deals with order of priority for grant where the Deceased left a will. r.22 specifies the order of priority in case of intestacy

9 See also *Burrows v HM Coroner for Preston [2008] EWHC 1387 (QB)* and *ND v LD*

In *ND v LD*[10] Judge Gareth Jones noted that although in *Holtham v Arnold*[11], the 'special circumstances', 'necessity' and 'expediency' required under s.116 were restricted to issues arising in the proper and efficient administration of the estate, following *Buchanan,* wider considerations can now be considered. In *Buchanan*, Hale J identified a number of relevant issues and noted that whether a particular combination of factors could amount to special circumstances "must in the end be a question of fact depending upon the nature of the alleged circumstances and the context in which they are raised."

How then have the courts decided the issue when faced with two or more parties with an equal right to the grant?

The Deceased in *Hartshorne v Gardner*[12] died intestate at the age of 44. His parents, who had divorced some 35 years prior to the accident, were equally entitled to the grant. The father wanted to bury the Deceased where the Deceased had lived, in Kington. The Deceased's mother wanted the Deceased cremated and his ashes interred where she lived, in Worcester. Worcester and Kington are some 40 miles apart. The body was under the authority of the coroner who refused to release it to either party without the agreement of the other or an order of the court.

Sonia Proudman QC considered the cases to which she had been referred, and formulated the following "helpful guidelines" as to the relevant factors to be taken into consideration:

i. the Deceased's wishes,

---

10 [2019] EWHC 3639 (Fam)

11 [1986] 2 BMLR

12 [2008] EWHC 3675

ii. the place with which the Deceased had the closest connection,

iii. the reasonable wishes and requirements of family and friends.

It was emphasised that the most important consideration is that the body be disposed of with all proper respect and decency, and if, possible, without further delay.

After hearing evidence, the Judge decided the issue in favour of the Claimant father on the basis that Kington was where the Deceased had made his life, and it was where the Deceased's brother, fiancée and friends were. The difficulty this would cause the Defendant mother in travelling to the grave was acknowledged, but the court found that in the last years of the Deceased's life, the Defendant had had very limited contact with the Deceased, and very little interest in the Deceased's personal life.

In *Anstey v Mundle*[13], where three daughters and a niece of the Deceased, all of whom were entitled to a grant either pursuant to the (contested) will or on intestacy, disagreed as to whether the Deceased should be buried in England or Jamaica, Jonathan Klein followed *Hartshorne* and said that the factors to be considered were

i. the Deceased's wishes,

ii. the reasonable requirements and wishes of the family who were left to grieve,

iii. the location with which the Deceased was most closely connected, and

---

13 [2016] EWHC 1073

iv. perhaps the most important, that the body be disposed of with all proper respect and decency, and if, possible, without further delay.

Having heard evidence, Judge Klein concluded that the Deceased should be buried in Jamaica with a particularly weighty factor being that this was held to be the Deceased's wish. To address the court's concerns as to the practicality of a burial in Jamaica, it was also ordered that a provision was to be inserted into the order which would allow the parties to return to court in the event that the burial had not occurred by a specified date.

Judge Proudman's helpful guidelines were also followed by Judge Mark Cawson QC in *Jakimaviciut v HM Coroner for Westminster*[14], although he noted that the criteria to be applied in deciding to whom a body ought to be released is likely to vary from case to case.

Court imposing own directions

There is conflicting authority as to whether the court can not only appoint a Personal Representative to make the arrangements for the proper disposal of the body and any attendant funeral, but whether it can also give directions as to the method of disposal and the manner in which any funeral should be held. In *Anstey v Mundle*[15], Jonathan Klein said that he did not think that the court can determine or direct where or how the Deceased should be buried; what the court can do is direct who has the power and duty to properly dispose of the Deceased[16]. In *Re JS*, Jackson J referred to *Anstey* and said that "the role of the court is not to give directions for the disposal of the

14 [2019] 10 WLUK 523

15 [2016] EWHC 1073 (Ch)

16 at paragraph 47

body but to resolve disagreement about who may make the arrangements"[17]. However, in *Oldham Metropolitan Borough Council v Makin*[18], which was concerned with how the body of the Moors Murderer, Ian Brady, should be dealt with, the Chancellor, Sir Geoffrey Vos, referred to *Grandison v Nembhard*[19] and *Hartshorne v Gardner*[20] and found that the court had inherent jurisdiction to give directions as to the method by which a body should be disposed of, and proceeded to give precise directions for the same, even down to the issue of whether music could be played during the cremation.

17 at paragraph 49

18 [2017] EWHC 2543 (Ch)

19 (1989) 4 BMLR 140

20 [2008] EWHC 3675 (Ch)

CHAPTER FIVE
FUNERAL AND DISPOSAL DISPUTES

As was seen in Chapter 2, there is no property in a body. One of the consequences of this, is that a Testator cannot dispose of his/her body by will, and therefore cannot leave legally binding directions as to how his/her body should be disposed of after death[1]. Just as the duty to dispose of the body allows the Personal Representative to call for possession of the body[2], the duty also gives the Personal Representative the right to decide how the body should be disposed of, and to make the necessary funeral arrangements; "where a man dies possessed of personal property, the duty of burying his body falls primarily on his Personal Representatives"[3].

It can therefore be seen that where there is a dispute over the method of disposal or the funeral arrangements, the question to ask is 'who has the obligation to properly dispose of the body?'[4]

Once a Personal Representative has established their right to dispose of a body, their discretion in this matter will not be interfered with by the court unless the Personal Representative has acted unreasonably:

> "To my mind it is plain that even if the performance of the executor's duty is capable of being controlled at the suit of a relative, the executor must have a discretion as to the mode and

---

1 *Williams v. Williams* (1881) 20 Ch. 659. Although see the commentary relating to the Human Tissue Act 2004 in chapter 2

2 See Chapter 2

3 Rees v Hughes (1946) KB 517

4 See Chapter 1

> place for the disposal of the corpse of the Deceased and that on ordinary principles the court will not interfere with the exercise of that discretion unless it is exercised in a way which shows that he has not properly weighed the factors which ought to have been taken into account in that it is wholly unreasonable."[5]

In *ND v LD*[6], Judge Gareth Jones said:

> "In general, I do not believe that I should micro-manage the funeral arrangements which are so intimately connected with family life and in this instance by parental ties. Public taste and convention in the organisation of funerals or cremations is constantly evolving, and a court should be slow to direct where or how a deceased would be buried. (I refer there to *Anstey v Mundle*). One can always envisage an extreme case where respect and decency was being totally disregarded and intervention might be required, but I have no reason to conclude that what is proposed by the father crosses that line. The burial at (Cemetery X), or the use of a horse drawn hearse, is not of itself exceptional. … I have no real evidence to conclude that decency, respect or public order would be compromised by what is proposed by the father."

The court has, however, intervened in funeral arrangements where it was felt necessary and in the public interest. *Oldham Metropolitan Borough Council v Makin*[7], was concerned with how the body (and subsequently the ashes) of the Moors Murderer, Ian Brady, should be dealt with, and in particular whether a certain piece of music should be played during the cremation. The Chancellor, Sir Geoffrey Vos, noted that although a Personal Representative had a duty to

---

5 *Grandison v Nembhard* 4 BMLR 140

6 [2019] EWHC 3639 (Fam)

7 [2017] EWHC 2543 (Ch)

dispose properly of a body, there was no obligation for a funeral to be held; "A funeral, as I pointed out in argument, is a ceremony. One definition is "a ceremony or service held shortly after a person's death, usually including the person's burial or cremation"."

Having found that it was necessary to make an order under s.116, giving administration of the estate to a third party for the purposes of disposing of the body, Vos C proceeded to consider whether the court had the power to give detailed directions for the disposal of the body;

> "80 In my judgment, the court does have an inherent jurisdiction to direct how the body of a deceased person should be disposed of. The court will normally, as I have said, be deciding between the competing wishes of different sets of relatives, and will only need to decide who should be responsible for disposal rather than what method of disposal should be employed. I cannot see, however, why the court's inherent jurisdiction over estates is not sufficiently extensive to allow it, in a proper case, to give directions as to the method by which a deceased's body should be disposed of. In my view, it is. Moreover, I am, for the reasons I have given in relation to section 116, prepared to exercise that jurisdiction in this case.
>
> ...
>
> 84 I have, therefore, determined that in the extremely unusual circumstances of this case, I should direct precisely how the deceased's body is to be disposed of. I shall even need to decide whether music can be played during the cremation."

It is noted that previous cases have indicated that the court does not have the authority to specify how a body should be disposed of, or how a funeral should be conducted. In *Anstey v Mundle*[8], Jonathan Klein said that he did not think that the court can determine or direct where or how the Deceased should be buried; what the court can do is direct who has the power and duty to properly dispose of the Deceased[9], and in *Re JS*, Jackson J referred to *Anstey* and said that "the role of the court is not to give directions for the disposal of the body but to resolve disagreement about who may make the arrangements"[10]. It must however be remembered that the order of Vos C, prescribing how the cremation should be conducted, including making orders relating to music, flowers and attendees, and as to how the ashes should be disposed of, arose in very unusual circumstances, and are unlikely to be required in many cases.

When arranging the disposal and funeral, there is no obligation upon a Personal Representative to abide by the wishes of the Deceased, although these should be taken into consideration. As Jackson J confirmed in *Re JS (A child) (Disposal of Body: Prospective Orders)*[11];

> "in English law, there is no right to dictate the treatment of one's body after death. This is so regardless of testamentary capacity or religion. The wishes of the deceased are relevant, perhaps highly so, but are not determinative and cannot bind third parties."

In *Burrows v HM Coroner for Preston*[12] Cranston J found that, following jurisprudence from the European Courts of Human Rights, the common law rule that the views of a deceased person can be

8 [2016] EWHC 1073 (Ch)

9 at paragraph 47

10 at paragraph 49

11 [2016] EWHC 2859 (Fam)

12 [2008] EWHC 1387 (QB) also reported as *Borrows v HM Coroner for Preston*

ignored, "is no longer good law"[13]. This assertion was, however, disputed in *Ibuna v Arroyo*[14] where Peter Smith J said:

> "It seems to me that the established law is correctly summarised by Hale J as she then was in ***Buchanan*** which gives the executor the primary duty to dispose of the body. In disposing of the body the executor is entitled to have regard to the expression made by the deceased but is not bound by them. Given that principle in my view there is no room further for any application of any human rights concepts to protect the right of the body to speak from death as it were"[15]

The comments of Jackson J in *Re JS* post-date both *Burrows* and *Ibuna*, and can therefore be taken to reflect the correct interpretation of the rights of the Deceased *vis a vis* his/her own wishes for disposal and funeral.

13 at paragraph 20

14 [2012] EWHC 428 (Ch)

15 at paragraph 50

CHAPTER SIX
ASHES AND CREMATION

The case usually cited as the authority that there is no property in a dead body, and that a Testator's instructions as to how his/her body should be disposed of are not binding upon a Personal Representative, is *Williams v Williams*[1], which is a case about cremation. In *Williams*, the Deceased left a codicil directing his executors to give his body to his friend, to be dealt with in such manner as he had directed to be done in a private letter to her. The Deceased further directed that any costs or expenses that might be incurred by the friend in carrying out the Deceased's wishes should be paid by the Deceased's executors. The Deceased's private instructions were for his body to be cremated, which in 1881 was not common, and in fact the court left the question as to whether or not it was lawful to burn a dead body unanswered. The court held that the direction within the codicil to the executors to deliver the property to the friend could not be enforced in law, and was therefore void, with the result that the friend did not recover the expenses she had incurred in having the body exhumed and flown to Italy where it had been cremated.

Cremation of a body is governed by statute[2]. At first instance in *R (Ghai) v Newcastle City Council*[3], Cranston J said:

> "In my view, then, the combined effect of the legislation and attendant regulations is plain: a cremation is the burning of human remains (regulation 2(1) of the 2008 Regulations); all cremations must take place in a crematorium (regulation 13); a

1 (1882) 20 Ch. D. 659

2 see Cremation Act 1902 and 1952 and associated Regulations

3 [2009] EWHC 978 (Admin); [2010] EWCACiv 59

> crematorium is a building (section 2 of the 1902 Act); and the burning of human remains other than in accordance with the provisions of the 2008 Regulations is a criminal offence: section 8 of the 1902 Act. Thus the burning of human remains, other than in a building, such as on an open air pyre, is an offence[4]."

On appeal as to the question of whether a cremation which accorded with the Applicant's religious beliefs (disposal of the body by traditional fire where sunlight could shine directly on the body) could reasonably be achieved in a structure which could be defined as a "building" within the meaning of the Act, Lord Neuberger said:

> "The combined effect of the Act and the Regulations is, therefore, that a cremation can only lawfully take place in a structure (i) which is a building, reading regulation 13 together with section 2, (ii) which has been constructed in a location which satisfies section 5, (iii) which is fitted with appliances for the purpose of burning human remains, pursuant to section 2, and (iv) whose opening . . . has been notified to the Secretary of State, under regulation 13. (Whether the Act, on its own, excludes cremation outside a crematorium does not call for decision in this case, at any rate at this stage: on a strictly literal reading, there may be a case for saying that it does not, but a more purposive reading could well justify a different result.)[5]"

An application for cremation must be made by way of the prescribed forms by either an executor or a "near relative" who is aged 16 or over[6]. A "near relative" is defined as a widow(er) or surviving civil

---

4 At paragraph 83

5 At paragraph 10

6 The Cremation (England and Wales) Regulations 2008 (2008/2841), Regulations 14 and 15

partner, a parent or child, or any other relative usually residing with the Deceased. An application may only be made by some other person if the medical referee is satisfied that the applicant is a proper person to make the application, and with the reason given for the application not being made by an executor or near relative. The prescribed form, which must be verified by a statement of truth, requires an applicant who is not an executor or near relative to confirm whether there are any executors or near relatives who have not been informed of the proposed cremation, their details, and the reason they have not been informed.

Following the cremation, the cremation authority either (i) must dispose of the ashes in accordance with the applicant's instructions, or (ii) where there are no instructions or the ashes are not collected in accordance with those instructions, may dispose of the ashes by burying or scattering the same. Where ashes are left temporarily in the care of the cremation authority, the ashes may not be interred or scattered unless the authority has made reasonable attempts to give the applicant 14 days' notice of their intention to do so. In "exceptional circumstances", the cremation authority may, at their discretion, release the ashes to someone other than the applicant or the applicant's nominee.[7]

Two difficulties arise from the prescribed procedure for the organisation of the cremation and the subsequent disposal of the ashes by the cremation authority. The first is that there may be a wide category of people falling within the definition of executors or near relative, but there is no mechanism for determining whose wishes should prevail in the event of a dispute. The second is that, barring exceptional circumstances, the cremation authority must give the ashes to the applicant, or dispose of them in accordance with the

7 The Cremation (England and Wales) Regulations 2008 (2008/2841), Regulation 30

applicant's instructions. However, the applicant may not necessarily be the person who has the ultimate right to decide how the ashes are disposed of.

Surprisingly, there is very little case law in relation to these matters. So far as any dispute over who should be the applicant is concerned, I would suggest that the person who has been determined to have the right to make the decision as to how the body should be disposed of should be the person with the final authority to decide this issue[8]. Ultimately of course, this is the person who is entitled to call for possession of the body so as to deliver the body to the crematorium, so as a matter of practicality, it is likely that this is the person who will be able to control whether, when, and how the cremation shall proceed.

In relation to the issue as to who has the final say over how the ashes are dealt with, the matter is not so clear cut. It is often suggested that as ashes are the remains of a body, the person with the duty to deal with the body also has the duty, and therefore the right, to deal with the ashes, to ensure that the "body" is properly disposed of. It is also noted that in canon law, there is no difference between the ashes of a cremated body and a corpse in relation to disinterment[9]. This was the basis of the decision of the Australian case of *Robinson v Pinegrove Memorial Park Ltd*[10] where Waddell CJ in Eq said:

> "...it is my view that an executor has a right to possession of the ashes of a deceased who has been cremated to direct how they shall finally be disposed of and that this right will be supported by a court, particularly where the executor intends to act in

---

8 see Chapter 1

9 *Re Atkins* [1989] 1 ALL ER 14 and *Re Church Norton Churchyard* [1989] 3 W.L.R. 272

10 (1986) 7 BPR 15,097

> accordance with the wishes of the deceased. I reach this conclusion by way of analogy from the rule of the general law that an executor has a right to possession of the corpse of the deceased for the purpose of its lawful disposal by burial or cremation or otherwise, which right, it seems to me, should be taken to extend to the ultimate disposal of the remains."

Robinson was cited in a later Australian case of *Leeburn*[11] where the Supreme Court of Victoria presided over a dispute between sibling executors over the ashes of their deceased father. Due to a disagreement as to how the ashes should be dealt with after the cremation, two of the siblings retrieved the ashes from the crematorium and caused them to be buried in a cemetery, without informing the Claimant. Two years later, the Claimant commenced an action asking for the ashes to be disinterred and divided into three portions. In dismissing the application Byrne J referred to *Robinson* but said that insofar as the Judge approached the question as being analogous to the right of an executor to dispose of the uncremated body, there were a number of points to note. The first was that with a burial, the executors discharge their obligation by having the body buried. The body then becomes part of the land in which it is buried and therefore it becomes part of the real estate held by the cemetery trust. The executors have no further function to perform and no further interest in the remains. Their only interest may be in the contract entered into with the cemetery trust under which the body is accepted for burial. However, with ashes, an executor is not bound to bury the same; they may be retained, scattered, or divided and the different portions disposed of differently. Byrne J then said:

> "Moreover, so long as they are not dispersed or otherwise lose their physical character as ashes, they may be owned and possessed. To my mind, therefore, it is apt to characterise the legal

11 [2004] VSC 172

> status of the ashes as similar to that of the preserved body in *Doodeward v Spence*[12]. In this way the application of fire to the cremated body is to be seen as the application to it of work or skill which has transformed it from flesh and blood to ashes, from corruptible material to material which is less so. The legal consequence of this accords with what I apprehend to be the community attitude and practice. Ashes which have in this way been preserved in specie are the subject of ordinary rights of property, subject to one possible qualification. In this way, ownership in the ashes may pass by sale or gift or otherwise. The only qualification, which, if it exists, may require some working out, arises from the fact that the ashes are, after all, the remains of a human being and for that reason they should be treated with appropriate respect and reverence."

Byrne J then went on to consider the legal interest of the executors in the ashes, holding that the ashes did not form part of the Deceased's estate and therefore did not pass under the will. Instead Byrne J concluded that the executors held the ashes as trustees for the "purpose of disposing or dealing with them in a way that seems to them to be appropriate having regard to any direction of the deceased in the will or otherwise and having regard to the claims of the relatives or others with an interest."

The conclusion reached by Byrne J, that the process of cremation has the result of transforming the ashes into property, was followed by DJ Marin in *DP v JCP*[13]. This case involved the application by one sibling to be appointed a financial deputy for P, her father, who had dementia. During the proceedings the other siblings (who opposed the application) discovered that the applicant held the ashes of their mother who had died and been cremated in 2007. The question

12 [1908] HCA 45; (1908) 6 CLR 406 at 412, per Griffith CJ.

13 [2010] COP 11692737

arose as to whether the ashes were the property of P. If they were, then the issue of who became P's Deputy was important, as that person would have control of the ashes. P had been appointed the executor of his wife's will, and had had capacity at the time of her death. However, probate had been granted, several months later, to the applicant with will annexed, for the use and benefit of P.

Considering the issue of the ashes, DJ Marin said:

> "51.I do not accept the suggestion that the effect of regulation 16 of the Cremation Regulations 1930[14] is to give some legal basis to [the applicant's] possession of the ashes. My view is that these regulations simply cater for the administrative act of ensuring that the cremation authority has someone to whom they may lawfully hand over the ashes. Without such a provision, the authority would have to retain ashes in every case which would make no sense.
>
> 52. Second, it is clear that the disposal of [the wife's] body fell to her executor.
>
> 53. Third, I do not accept the proposition that after cremation, the executor's role comes to an end. I prefer to follow the reasoning of Byrne J in Leeburn and say that the

14 "16. After the cremation of the remains of a deceased person the ashes shall be given into the charge of the person who applied for the cremation if he so desires. If not, they shall be retained by the Cremation Authority and, in the absence of any special arrangement for their burial or preservation, they shall either be decently interred in a burial ground or in land adjoining the crematorium reserved for the burial of ashes, or shall be scattered thereon. In the case of ashes left temporarily in the charge of the cremation authority and not removed within a reasonable time, a fortnight's notice shall be given to the person who applied for the cremation before the remains are interred or scattered."

> executor holds the ashes on trust for the purposes of the family disposing of them.
>
> 54. Fourth, the fact that [the applicant] placed [the wife's] ashes in an urn that she says she purchased does not automatically mean that she acquired possession of them. It is necessary to examine how the ashes came to be placed into the urn before reaching a conclusion. It is possible that ashes are contained in an urn for safekeeping pending a decision by the executor as to their disposal."

In this case, the court did not have sufficient evidence to determine what should happen to the ashes, and this was left to the panel deputy to be appointed. However, DJ Marin did say that

> "if [the applicant] arranged the funeral on behalf of P acting as executor, then [the applicant] holds the ashes on trust for the family for the purposes of disposing of them. If P gave the ashes to [the applicant] on the basis that P wanted her to have them forever, then the ashes will belong to [the applicant]. If P gave the ashes to [the applicant] without saying that he wanted [the applicant] to keep them forever, then it is probable that P gave them to [the applicant] as executor and [the applicant] therefore holds them on trust for the family in her capacity as executrix. If the cremation was after [the applicant] was granted probate, then as executrix [the applicant] holds the ashes on trust for the family."

It can therefore be seen that even if one person has been designated the Personal Representative for the purposes of disposal of the body, this may not solve the issue of what should happen to the ashes if the Personal Representative is now the trustee of the ashes and the 'beneficiaries' all have different ideas as to what should happen to the ashes.

In the case of *Fessi v Whitmore*[15], an ashes dispute was determined on the basis that the court was being asked to resolve a dispute between two trustees. M was a 12 year-old child who died in an accident only a few days after moving with his father to a new home near Aberystwth. M had lived with his father since his parents' divorce, but until this move had stayed in the Nuneaton area, where the family had always lived. The father wished M's ashes to be interred near the new home, where he could tend the grave, while the mother wished M's ashes to be in Nuneaton. The father claimed that, as the main carer for M after the breakdown of the marriage, his wishes should prevail. The mother argued that in view of the very brief time M had spent in the new home, Nuneaton was the best place for his ashes to be laid to rest. In deciding in favour of Nuneaton, Judge Boggis QC noted that there had been an issue as to the jurisdiction of the court. The case had started as a Children Act application, and then proceeded under Ord 85 (which would now be an application under CPR 64) as an action for the administration under the direction of the court of an estate or the execution under the direction of the court of a trust. Judge Boggis QC said that he had his doubts as to whether this was the appropriate vehicle as "this is not a case of a difficulty in the administration of an estate. This is a valid dispute between parents as to the final resting-place of the remains of their child. What, in my judgment, I am being asked to do is to adjudicate upon that valid dispute raised between persons having a like entitlement to the remains of Mark and to decide between the two conflicting proposals for the future of his ashes. It seems to me that, on analysis, the parties are rather in the nature of trustees bringing a dispute to the court and seeking the directions of the court as to the resolution of that dispute, given that there are valid contentions on both sides. It is on that basis that I propose to decide the case. I do not think I am being asked to give directions as to the administration of an estate. I am being asked to decide between the conflicting argu-

15 [1999] 1 FLR 767

ments of equally entitled parents as to the way in which Mark's ashes should be disposed of and I do that on the usual basis that this court is well used to exercising discretion in disputes between trustees and adjudicating on the proper course to follow when no agreement can be reached by the parties concerned. One takes all of the background into account. One takes into account the views held on both sides and comes to a conclusion which does fairness and justice to both sides."

A further issue arose in *Fessi* when it was proposed by the father that one solution was that the ashes should be split. In circumstances where the mother did not agree to this course of action, Judge Boggis QC rejected this course of action on the basis that it was "wholly inappropriate". It is however noted that there is nothing to prevent the ashes from being divided where all parties consent.

CHAPTER SEVEN
EXHUMATION OF BODIES AND ASHES

Once a body or ashes have been buried, any disinterment or other disturbance of the same, without lawful authority, is an offence both at common law and by statute[1]. Authority for disinterment can be granted by way of a licence from the Secretary of State, or via a faculty from the consistory court where the body is interred in consecrated ground of the Anglican church. A coroner who requires a body for the purposes of investigating or providing evidence as to the cause of death may issue a signed direction for the exhumation of a body[2].

In *R. (on the application of Rudewicz) v Ministry of Justice*[3], an appeal was brought against a refusal to grant a judicial review of the decision of the Secretary of State for Justice to grant a licence to permit the exhumation of the remains of a Priest so that he could be transferred to a cemetery two miles away. In dismissing the appeal, the Master of the Rolls noted that section 25(ii) of the Burial Act 1857 appeared to confer an unfettered discretion on the Secretary of State, and that the practice of granting a licence where it is requested by the next of kin for the purpose of re-interment elsewhere was not unreasonable.

> "The common law offence is committed where a person carries out an exhumation without lawful authority, and section 25(ii) empowers the Secretary of State to give such authority by means of a licence. I cannot see any reason why such a licence should be relatively hard to obtain simply because, in its

1 Section 25 of the Burial Act 1857

2 The Coroners (Investigations) Regulations 2013, Regulation 22

3 [2012] EWCA Civ 499

> absence, the act it authorises would be a crime. If anything, one would have thought that that would justify it being relatively easy to obtain a licence.
>
> As for the approach of the consistory courts to faculties for exhumation, I do not consider that it is applicable to the standard to be adopted by the Secretary of State to the grant of licences under section 25(ii). The reasons for the 'general presumption of permanence' adopted by the consistory courts was explained in *Blagdon* [2002] Fam 299, paras 23–27, as being based on the 'theology of burial'. That theology is plainly highly relevant to the faculty jurisdiction, but it is equally plainly irrelevant to the exercise of the secular power in section 25(ii)."

Detailed consideration of when a faculty will be granted and the procedure surrounding the same is beyond the scope of this work. However, as was referred to in *Rudewicz*, where a body has been buried in consecrated ground pursuant to a Christian burial, there is a presumption of permanence, and a faculty will only be granted in exceptional circumstances[4].

At paragraphs 33 and 35 of *Blagdon*, the Arches Court of Canterbury said

> "33. We have concluded that there is much to be said for reverting to the straightforward principle that a faculty for exhumation will only be exceptionally granted. Exceptional means 'forming an exception' . . . and guidelines can assist in identifying various categories of exception. Whether the facts in a particular case warrant a finding that the case is to be

4 *In Re Blagdon cemetary* [2002] Fam 299

treated as an exception is for the chancellor to determine on the balance of probabilities.

35. We consider that it should always be made clear that it is for the petitioner to satisfy the consistory court that there are special circumstances in his/her case which justify the making of an exception from the norm that Christian burial, that is, burial of a body or cremated remains in a consecrated churchyard or consecrated part of a local authority cemetery, is final. It will then be for the chancellor to decide whether the petitioner has so satisfied him/her."

In *In re Camp's petition, In re St Mark's Churchyard, Fairfield*[5], the petitioner sought a faculty for the exhumation and reinterment of his father's cremated remains in the family plot of a churchyard in an area where the family had lived for over 300 years. In granting the faculty, Fookes Dep Ch noted that although in both *In re Christ Church, Alsager*[6] and *In re Blagdon Cemetery*[7] the appeal courts emphasised that the normal rule is that burial in consecrated land is permanent, and that a faculty will only exceptionally be granted for exhumation, these cases did not go further than requiring reasons for providing an exception.

In *In Re Fairmile Cemetery, Lower Assendon*[8], the petitioner had secured the exclusive right to be buried in a particular plot in the cemetery. As a result of admitted administrative errors by the burial authority, the family of M was subsequently also granted the exclusive right of burial to the plot, and the body of M was buried there. The petitioner sought a faculty for the exhumation and rein-

5 [2013] PTSR 953

6 [1999] Fam 142

7 [2002] Fam 299

8 [2017] Fam. 349

terment of M's remains, which was opposed by M's family. Refusing the faculty, it was held that there was no rule, or even a presumption, that exhumation would be permitted or readily granted where a mistake as to the location of a grave had been made. The permanence of Christian burial was predicated upon the disposal of remains in the intended plot or grave, so that where a body was deposited in an unintended grave, the law did not presume that burial to be permanent, and there was no presumption against exhumation for a petitioner to overcome. However where, as in this case, a body had been buried in the place where those concerned with the arrangements for the burial intended it should be buried, the burial was presumed to be permanent and a petitioner therefore had to overcome that presumption of permanence in order to be granted a faculty. The remedy for breach of the exclusive burial right was through the Local Government Ombudsman or by a claim for damages in the temporal courts.

In canon law, there is no difference between the ashes of a cremated body and a corpse in relation to disinterment[9], and therefore exceptional circumstances will also be needed for the exhumation of ashes.

9 *Re Atkins* [1989] 1 All ER 14 and *Church Norton Churchyard, Re* [1989] 3 WLR 272

CHAPTER EIGHT HEADSTONES AND MEMORIALS

This is not technically a dispute over a body, but this doesn't mean that disputes over headstones or other memorials are any less heated or emotive.

The authority of the Personal Representative in relation to a headstone or other monument or memorial is not as obvious as it is for a body. In *In re St John, Dipton*[1] it was said that where there was a dispute as to the type and wording of a memorial "the views of the executor should … be given weight although not to the same extent [as to the issue of exhumation]". It should also be remembered that as the cost of any headstone is often an estate expense, the consent of those who will be paying for the same (which will usually be the residuary beneficiaries) will need to be obtained.

Where a body is buried in a churchyard, the burial does not include a right for anyone to erect a memorial to the deceased. This issue was considered in *re St Augustine's Churchyard, Droitwich Spa*[2] where it was held that where a memorial was to be erected, there was no overriding legal principle to determine who should have the power to decide the manner in which a deceased person should be commemorated, if at all, and as there was no overwhelming need for a memorial to be erected, it was better that there be no memorial at all than one which was bitterly opposed by some who were closely connected with the deceased. In this case, the partner of the Deceased was unable to agree with the Deceased's children and grandchildren

1 [2011] PTSR D29

2 [2016] 1 WLR 3365

on the design of a headstone to be erected above the Deceased's grave in a consecrated churchyard. Due to the lack of agreement, the consistory court initially granted the archdeacon's petition for a simple memorial recording merely the deceased's full name and dates of birth and death, however, a compromise was subsequently agreed between the parties and the partner's petition in an agreed amended form was therefore granted.

Where a body or ashes are buried within a local authority graveyard, Article 10(1) of the Local Authorities' Cemeteries Order 1977 (SI 1977/204) provides:

> Grant of burial rights and rights to erect memorials, and agreements for maintenance of graves and memorials
>
> 10.—(1) A burial authority may grant, on such terms and subject to such conditions as they think proper—
>
> (a) to any person—
>
> (i) the exclusive right of burial in any grave space or grave, or the right to construct a walled grave or vault together with the exclusive right of burial therein; or
>
> (ii) the right to one or more burials in any grave space or grave which is not subject to any exclusive right of burial;
>
> (b) to the owner of a right described in (a)(i) or (ii) (or to any person who satisfies them that he is a relative of a person buried in the grave or vault, or is acting at the request of such a relative and that it is impractical for him, or such relative, to trace the owner of the right so described), the right to place and maintain, or to put any additional inscription on, a tomb-

stone or other memorial on the grave space, grave or vault in respect of which the right so described subsists;

(c) to any person, the right to place and maintain a memorial in a cemetery otherwise than on a grave space, grave or vault in respect of which a right described in (a)(i) has been granted, but—

(i) in the case of a memorial to be placed in a chapel provided as mentioned in article 6(1)(b), only at the request of persons appearing to the burial authority to be representative of the Church of England or other particular denomination or religious body at whose request the chapel was provided; and

(ii) in the case of any other memorial being an additional inscription on an existing memorial, only with the consent of the owner of the right to place and maintain such existing memorial.

The difficulties which can be caused by this Regulation were also considered in *In re St Augustine's Churchyard, Droitwich Spa* where it was noted that the effect of regulation 10(1) was that where a body or ashes have been buried, any person who satisfies the burial authority that he or she is a relative of the deceased may place a memorial on the grave. Mynors CH notes that there is no definition of 'relative' in the Order, and it is not clear how closely the person has to be related to the deceased, nor whether a person who had been living with the deceased up to the time of the death (or indeed at an earlier time) would be included. It is also noted that the Order is wholly silent on the question as to what is to be done where two relatives wish to place different memorials on a grave in such a cemetery.

> "43 In the absence of any clearly stated principle as to who has the right to decide the wording of a memorial, it may be helpful to consider briefly the general law as to rights and duties of executors and others in the event of a death.
>
> 44 The starting point appears to be that a person's rights cease at the moment of death. That is to say, the shroud or coffin containing a dead body (or, in the case of cremation, the casket containing the ashes of the deceased) cannot be owned by a dead person, and so must remain the property of the person who owned it immediately before they were put to use: see *Haynes's Case* (1613) 12 Co Rep 113. On that basis, the memorial to a dead person also remains the property of the person or persons who acquired it – rather than the heirs-at-law of the person commemorated. That conclusion is supported by the decision of the Peterborough Consistory Court in *In re St Andrew's, Thornhaugh* [1976] Fam 230 (considered in *In re St Mary's, Oldswinford* 17 Consistory and Commissary Court Cases, case 37). But that provides no guidance as to who has a right to place a memorial on a grave in the first place."

Having considered the rights of the Personal Representative in relation to the disposal of the body, Mynors CH concludes that

> "It therefore seems that, whereas the executors are given the power to decide as to the manner of the disposal of a dead body, there is no overriding legal principle to determine who should have the power to decide as to the manner in which a deceased person should be commemorated – if at all."

In the absence of the Personal Representative having an overriding right to determine disputes relating to graves and memorials, it is likely that an individual case will have to be decided after consideration of the rules and regulations of the particular graveyard. Many local authorities provide that an individual is able to purchase an Exclusive Right of Burial in a grave, and that the purchaser, or their Personal Representative, will thereafter be entitled to determine who can be buried in the grave and whether a memorial can be erected. Local Authorities also often provide that any memorials are approved by the Council, with a designated appeals process in the event of dispute.

In *In re West Norwood Cemetery*[3], P was registered as the owner of a burial plot in circumstances where P and his uncle had paid for the grave, and other family members had paid for associated expenses such as the interment fee and the casket. When a dispute arose as to who was the owner of the plot, the consistory court held that P held the exclusive burial rights on constructive trust for the family.

West Norwood was actually a case about exclusive burial rights in relation to authorising the interment of additional ashes in a grave. However, under cemetery rules and regulations, the person with the exclusive burial rights is often also the person with the right to erect a memorial, so in these circumstances, the court could determine any dispute over the headstone as a dispute between trustees and beneficiaries.

---

3 [2005] 1 W.L.R. 2176

CHAPTER NINE
COSTS

This is an issue which could really have been dealt with in a footnote or a paragraph, but it has been given its own chapter so it can be found easily given the importance of costs to most parties.

The rule is very simple; as was held by Jonathan Klein in *Anstey v Mundle*[1], litigation relating to disputes over bodies and ashes is "hostile litigation of the normal sort", and as such, costs will generally follow the event. Judge Klein specifically stated that he did not think that any of the special rules that apply in certain probate cases were analogous. Hoffman J had reached the same conclusion in *Holtham v Arnold*[2];

> "I have no doubt that both sides have acted out of what they consider to be moral duty and the position of both is therefore in that respect equal. But the practice of the court is that the side which loses pays the costs and therefore I feel that it would not be a proper exercise of my discretion to say anything other than that the plaintiff should pay the costs."

1 [2016] EWHC 1073

2 (1986) 2 BMLR 123

MORE BOOKS BY LAW BRIEF PUBLISHING

A selection of our other titles available now:-

'Covid-19, Homeworking and the Law – The Essential Guide to Employment and GDPR Issues' by Forbes Solicitors
'Covid-19, Force Majeure and Frustration of Contracts – The Essential Guide' by Keith Markham
'Covid-19 and Criminal Law – The Essential Guide' by Ramya Nagesh
'Covid-19 and Family Law in England and Wales – The Essential Guide' by Safda Mahmood
'Covid-19 and the Implications for Planning Law – The Essential Guide' by Bob Mc Geady & Meyric Lewis
'Covid-19, Residential Property, Equity Release and Enfranchisement – The Essential Guide' by Paul Sams and Louise Uphill
'Covid-19, Brexit and the Law of Commercial Leases – The Essential Guide' by Mark Shelton
'Covid-19 and the Law Relating to Food in the UK and Republic of Ireland – The Essential Guide' by Ian Thomas
'A Practical Guide to the General Data Protection Regulation (GDPR) – 2nd Edition' by Keith Markham
'Ellis on Credit Hire – Sixth Edition' by Aidan Ellis & Tim Kevan
'A Practical Guide to Working with Litigants in Person and McKenzie Friends in Family Cases' by Stuart Barlow
'Protecting Unregistered Brands: A Practical Guide to the Law of Passing Off' by Lorna Brazell
'A Practical Guide to Secondary Liability and Joint Enterprise Post-Jogee' by Joanne Cecil & James Mehigan

'A Practical Guide to the Pre-Action RTA Claims Protocol for Personal Injury Lawyers' by Antonia Ford
'A Practical Guide to Neighbour Disputes and the Law' by Alexander Walsh
'A Practical Guide to Forfeiture of Leases' by Mark Shelton
'A Practical Guide to Coercive Control for Legal Practitioners and Victims' by Rachel Horman
'A Practical Guide to Rights Over Airspace and Subsoil' by Daniel Gatty
'Tackling Disclosure in the Criminal Courts – A Practitioner's Guide' by Narita Bahra QC & Don Ramble
'A Practical Guide to the Law of Driverless Cars – Second Edition' by Alex Glassbrook, Emma Northey & Scarlett Milligan
'A Practical Guide to TOLATA Claims' by Greg Williams
'Artificial Intelligence – The Practical Legal Issues' by John Buyers
'A Practical Guide to the Law of Prescription in Scotland' by Andrew Foyle
'A Practical Guide to the Construction and Rectification of Wills and Trust Instruments' by Edward Hewitt
'A Practical Guide to the Law of Bullying and Harassment in the Workplace' by Philip Hyland
'How to Be a Freelance Solicitor: A Practical Guide to the SRA-Regulated Freelance Solicitor Model' by Paul Bennett
'A Practical Guide to Prison Injury Claims' by Malcolm Johnson
'A Practical Guide to the Small Claims Track' by Dominic Bright
'A Practical Guide to Advising Clients at the Police Station' by Colin Stephen McKeown-Beaumont
'A Practical Guide to Antisocial Behaviour Injunctions' by Iain Wightwick
'Practical Mediation: A Guide for Mediators, Advocates, Advisers, Lawyers, and Students in Civil, Commercial, Business, Property, Workplace, and Employment Cases' by Jonathan Dingle with John Sephton
'The Mini-Pupillage Workbook' by David Boyle

'A Practical Guide to Crofting Law' by Brian Inkster
'A Practical Guide to Spousal Maintenance' by Liz Cowell
'A Practical Guide to the Law of Domain Names and Cybersquatting' by Andrew Clemson
'A Practical Guide to the Law of Gender Pay Gap Reporting' by Harini Iyengar
'A Practical Guide to the Rights of Grandparents in Children Proceedings' by Stuart Barlow
'NHS Whistleblowing and the Law' by Joseph England
'Employment Law and the Gig Economy' by Nigel Mackay & Annie Powell
'A Practical Guide to Noise Induced Hearing Loss (NIHL) Claims' by Andrew Mckie, Ian Skeate, Gareth McAloon
'An Introduction to Beauty Negligence Claims – A Practical Guide for the Personal Injury Practitioner' by Greg Almond
'Intercompany Agreements for Transfer Pricing Compliance' by Paul Sutton
'Zen and the Art of Mediation' by Martin Plowman
'A Practical Guide to the SRA Principles, Individual and Law Firm Codes of Conduct 2019 – What Every Law Firm Needs to Know' by Paul Bennett
'A Practical Guide to Adoption for Family Lawyers' by Graham Pegg
'A Practical Guide to Industrial Disease Claims' by Andrew Mckie & Ian Skeate
'A Practical Guide to Redundancy' by Philip Hyland
'A Practical Guide to Vicarious Liability' by Mariel Irvine
'A Practical Guide to Applications for Landlord's Consent and Variation of Leases' by Mark Shelton
'A Practical Guide to Relief from Sanctions Post-Mitchell and Denton' by Peter Causton
'A Practical Guide to Equity Release for Advisors' by Paul Sams
'A Practical Guide to Unlawful Eviction and Harassment' by Stephanie Lovegrove
'A Practical Guide to the Law Relating to Food' by Ian Thomas

'A Practical Guide to Financial Services Claims' by Chris Hegarty
'The Law of Houses in Multiple Occupation: A Practical Guide to HMO Proceedings' by Julian Hunt
'A Practical Guide to Unlawful Eviction and Harassment' by Stephanie Lovegrove
'A Practical Guide to Solicitor and Client Costs' by Robin Dunne
'Occupiers, Highways and Defective Premises Claims: A Practical Guide Post-Jackson – 2nd Edition' by Andrew Mckie
'A Practical Guide to Financial Ombudsman Service Claims' by Adam Temple & Robert Scrivenor
'A Practical Guide to Advising Schools on Employment Law' by Jonathan Holden
'A Practical Guide to Running Housing Disrepair and Cavity Wall Claims: 2nd Edition' by Andrew Mckie & Ian Skeate
'A Practical Guide to Holiday Sickness Claims – 2nd Edition' by Andrew Mckie & Ian Skeate
'Arguments and Tactics for Personal Injury and Clinical Negligence Claims' by Dorian Williams
'A Practical Guide to QOCS and Fundamental Dishonesty' by James Bentley
'A Practical Guide to Drone Law' by Rufus Ballaster, Andrew Firman, Eleanor Clot
'A Practical Guide to Compliance for Personal Injury Firms Working With Claims Management Companies' by Paul Bennett
'A Practical Guide to the Landlord and Tenant Act 1954: Commercial Tenancies' by Richard Hayes & David Sawtell
'A Practical Guide to Dog Law for Owners and Others' by Andrea Pitt
'RTA Allegations of Fraud in a Post-Jackson Era: The Handbook – 2nd Edition' by Andrew Mckie
'RTA Personal Injury Claims: A Practical Guide Post-Jackson' by Andrew Mckie
'On Experts: CPR35 for Lawyers and Experts' by David Boyle
'An Introduction to Personal Injury Law' by David Boyle

'A Practical Guide to Chronic Pain Claims' by Pankaj Madan
'A Practical Guide to Claims Arising from Fatal Accidents' by James Patience
'A Practical Guide to Subtle Brain Injury Claims' by Pankaj Madan

www.ingramcontent.com/pod-product-compliance
Ingram Content Group UK Ltd.
Pitfield, Milton Keynes, MK11 3LW, UK
UKHW020151290926
15471UKWH00004B/815

9 781912 687985